PAST
SOMERSET
TIMES

ILLUSTRATED STUDIES
FROM THE COUNTY'S
RICH HISTORY
Volume 1

FIDUCIA PRESS

2004

PAST SOMERSET TIMES

ILLUSTRATED STUDIES FROM THE COUNTY'S RICH HISTORY

Geoffrey Body: editor, writer and photographer
Roy Gallop: designer, illustrator and contributor
Ken Griffiths: design associate and contributor
Tess Green: contributor:

Front cover: Background, 16th century map of Somerset
Title page: 'Conversation at a village pump'. This page: 'Post Chaise paying Toll'
Contemporary engravings by W H Pyne (1769 -1843).
Rear cover: For illustrations and engravings, see acknowledgements page 48.

Published by Fiducia Press, 10 Fairfield Road, Southville, Bristol, BS3 1LG, in association with Kingsmead Press.

FIDUCIA PRESS ISBN 0 946217 15 7
Printed in Great Britain by Doveton Press Ltd., of Bristol.

CONTENTS

INTRODUCTION

In 1923 the Society of Somerset Folk took the courageous step of launching the Somerset Year Book. Each issue provided a selection of pieces dealing with some of the highly interesting but rather less well-known aspects of the county's past. Events, incidents, people, places, customs, curiosities, crafts etc. all featured in successive annual issues, and all with the aim of providing informative and enjoyable reading for those expatriates who had a strong interest in the county. The success enjoyed by the Somerset Year Book is reflected in the fact that sixteen issues were published before the approaching war changed the world for everyone.

More recently the Somerset Magazine carried this mantle by including frequent articles on intriguing aspects of the past but the gap between general, generic and substantial works and the specialist works of learned organisations is now largely unfilled. Hence this book, which strives to be accurate, informative and enjoyable and regrets any shortcomings in any of these areas. The writers and publishers modestly hope that not only might it fulfil a need in the county but also prompt further information on the subjects included and a sufficient response to warrant further editions.

Frome Round Tower

Frome: 'the toune that standythe moste by clothinge'

The character of present-day Somerset still reflects some of the influence of a wide and prosperous trade in wool and cloth begun in the Middle Ages. So many of its churches were built, rebuilt or extended thanks to profits from sheep, and many attractive houses in the county originated as the homes of wealthy clothiers. Additionally, quite a few of the older factories and warehouses were once used by some branch or process of the textile industry, and many examples of workers' housing also survive.

Frome well exemplifies all this. The town was shaped by dramatic growth in the 18th and 19th centuries and many a British regiment raised to face the armies of Napoleon wore blue uniforms made of cloth produced in Frome. After dyeing with locally-grown woad the wool would have been dried around a cast iron central stove in a building like the one pictured. This particular one was built some time before 1796, when it was recorded as a scouring furnace where wool was dried after scouring to remove the lanolin content. Nicely restored some two hundred years later it now houses an extremely useful Tourist Information Centre.

Wife for Sale

'Her husband with her own consent sold her by publick auction with a rope round her waist in Chard market for half a crown'.

St. Thomas's Market, Bristol 1823.

In 18th and 19th century England there was a quite widespread misconception among poorer people that wife-selling was a legitimate way of dissolving an unrewarding marriage. Several hundred examples of the practice are recorded and Thomas Hardy gave it classic status when intoxicated hay-trusser Michael Henchard sold his wife for five guineas within the first dozen pages of *The Mayor of Casterbridge*. This was a spur of the moment incident but many wife 'sales' seem to have been prearranged to recognise a situation already brought about by disenchantment or infidelity. It was generally believed that for a separation to be 'legitimate' the sale had to have a degree of formality. The event had to take place in public, somewhere like a market place, a common or a fairground, the wife could expect to be led there with a halter round her neck or waist and there had to be witnesses, preferably of good standing. Sometimes an 'auctioneer' was present to conduct the affair and establish the price. The role of the auctioneer or principal witness was important and was sometimes taken by a local overseer or churchwarden with the sale recorded in the parish register to give it an added sense of being official.

In 19th century Somerset a wife was presented for auction at Farmborough, near Bath. The event took place at the Bell Inn and the 'victim' had to stand with a halter around her neck until the highest bid was reached and accepted. This was only a gallon of beer, although in other parts of the country wives had been known to command their weight in the local brew. Apparently the Farmborough transaction was not considered to be complete until the buyer carried his prize over the threshold of her new home as this ended her right to veto the sale.

There was an even more curious affair further south in 1814 when Thomas Tuffen of Henstridge sold his wife, apparently as part of a business deal! The Tuffens sold ginger-bread at local markets and fairs but at Stalbridge market Thomas went a bit further and sold his wife as well as their basket of stock! In a halter, she was handed over to sawyer Joseph Cains and led of to her new home. No price is recorded.

When Elizabeth Phillips was sold here for half a crown, Chard's main street housed a market, butchers' shambles and a 16th century guildhall.

The wife of one Brassy Kime fetched only eighteen pence in Lincolnshire but when Joseph Phillips sold his wife Elizabeth to Henry Morris at Chard Market around the year 1805 he did get half a crown for her. They had married at Chaffcombe less than two years previously but soon after their son was born Joseph moved out and went to live in Chard. Six months later his wife moved in with Henry Morris on the northern edge of that town. It appears that all three agreed to the public sale which then took place and, indeed, remained the best of friends. Certainly Elizabeth continued to see a great deal of her first partner, even registering children in his name in 1806 and 1809. However she had a large family with Henry and remained faithful while he was in the militia, the situation being finally regularised after many years when Elizabeth and Henry married in Chard church in 1839, two months after Joseph's death. The local paper reported that the marriage took place 'under circumstances which do not every day occur' and labelled the event as 'better late than never'.

By this time the going price for wives had risen appreciably judging by the case of lath-maker Simon Mitchell of Taunton. After seven years of marriage he sold his wife Sarah around 1830 to James Larcombe of Curry Rivel for two sovereigns. James was 15 years older than his expensive 'bride' but the couple settled down together in Westover, where James made a living as a shoemaker, and got on well enough to produce ten children together, all taking the Mitchell surname. Sadly, age and poverty later overtook James and Sarah, he being recorded as a Langport pauper while she eked out a living as a washer-woman in Taunton, that being the place of her legal husband's settlement.

Despite these and other examples of wife-selling at places as far apart as Canterbury (1820) and Carlisle (1832) and at least as late as 1859 (Dudley), the process did not always go smoothly as a Yorkshire example of 1837 shows. A man tried there for attempting to sell his wife got an unexpected separation in the form of a month's imprisonment. Exactly who brought the charge against him is not recorded!

And drover John Nash must have regretted the impulse that led to him offering his wife for sale at St Thomas's Market in Bristol in 1823. This was one of the city's traditional markets, situated between St Thomas's Church and Bristol Bridge, and here on 29 May of that year he led his wife into the busy area opposite the Bell Yard in a neck halter. Catching the attention of the crowd, he boldly proclaimed that Mrs Nash was for sale to the highest bidder. This announcement produced a stunned silence with no offers forth-coming until one young man, probably to ease the unhappy woman's embarrassment, timidly offered a bid of 6d. Indignantly Nash demanded a better offer, emphasising that his wife was 'sound and free from vice' and worth a good deal more.

No one else wanted to get involved, it seemed, so the drover eventually accepted the offered bid of sixpence. However, the prospective purchaser was, by now, deeply regret-ting ever having made it. So much so that he quickly re-offered the new 'bride' his reck-less gesture had brought him and thankfully accepted an improved figure of 9d. But the lady had other ideas and ran off with her mother, hotly pursued by her latest purchaser. She had clearly had enough of the whole business and resisted his claim that he was the successful bidder and that she must now go with him, insisting that she would only do so if a magistrate ordered her to. One was found and, to the lady's relief, promptly dismissed the case. Mrs Nash was now free but the crowd had found the whole spectacle distaste-ful and turned angrily on Nash driving him from the scene only 6d better off for his unsavoury conduct. In contrast the Quixotic young man had made of profit of 3d from his kindness and Mrs Nash no longer had to share her life with a herd of sheep or cattle. A piece of contemporary verse observed:-

> *Come all you kind husbands who have scolding wives,*
> *Who tho' living together are tired of your lives,*
> *If you cannot persuade her nor good natur'd make her,*
> *Place a rope round her neck & to market pray take her.*

Giants and Dwarfs

*Of Miss Hold of Crewkerne it was recorded 'her immense
stature measures nearly seven feet, commanding a
prepossessing figure beyond description'.*

Somerset's early history does not feature as many giants as the more rugged counties such as Cornwall but legend does credit them with a major involvement in the creation of Bristol's Avon Gorge and with throwing huge boulders around in the Porlock area. Legend also has it that a giant wizard once lived among the caves on the hillside above Loxton and this may have some connection with the discovery of an unusual skeleton during the digging of a grave in the churchyard there. With no coffin, the head rested on a square stone and the body measured 6ft 3ins excluding the lower legs and feet which were too deeply embedded to measure. At Dunster Castle a tall skeleton was found manacled to the gatehouse while the 15th century memorial to Sir John St Loe in Chew Magna church represents him as over 7ft tall.

During the course of sinking a well at Wedmore in 1670 some startling remains were revealed at a depth of 13ft. They were taken to be those of an early giant for the top of the skull was an inch thick and a single tooth measured 3ins in length. Broken off, the same tooth was said to be 3.25ins round and to weigh 3.5ozs, but there do have to be serious doubts about these measurements. Less open to question is the 1886 photograph of local child Ernest Middleton which is held in Porlock museum. At one year old Ernest is said to have been 3ft tall, to have had a 30in chest and to have weighed 58lb.

Taunton has been associated with both giants and dwarfs. A Miss Widdicombe of that town was claimed to be 'the most impressive female dwarf phenomenon ever presented to the public.' Patronised by the Royal Family in 1819, this tiny lady was only 2ft 11ins tall and could, apparently, bend her fingers backwards to touch the elbow. At the other end of the scale a giantess had been exhibited at the Assize Fair at Taunton eight years earlier while a Somerset girl of 6ft 10ins made an appearance at London's Bartholomew Fair in 1825. Said to have been 16-year old Elizabeth Stock, her 'act' included inviting the largest man in her audience to place his booted foot in her slipper.

A giant who was born in Lincolnshire in 1805 was shown so much kindness in Taunton that he expressed a wish to be buried there and was duly interred at St Mary Magdalene Church in July 1829. He was Joseph Neal Sewell who grew to a height of 7ft 4ins and weighed 37 stone. Typhus robbed young Joseph of his sight during his early years in South Wales, but he made a living from public exhibition at Bristol, Taunton and Exeter, where he lived in a caravan as part of Bromsgrove's Menagerie. Bromsgrove himself was a Taunton innkeeper and was one of those who arranged the burial of his huge friend who feared his body might be used for anatomical research after his death. Sewell wore size 15 shoes and needed 17 yards of cloth for his coat, waistcoat and trousers. His exhibition companion was a Somerset-born dwarf named Farnham.

A grave here, beside St Mary Magdalene Church at Taunton, was the final resting place of 7ft 4in giant Joseph Sewell. It was unmarked for fear of disturbance.

Some accounts mention a giantess from the Crewkerne area but the Somerset height record surely belongs to the two-headed, 12ft tall Patagonian giant whose preserved body was on show at Weston-super-Mare's Grand Pier for many years. The story of Kap Dwa who was born in the middle of the 17th century, captured by Spanish sailors and exhibited in a glass case after his death, is one of complexity and uncertainty until a Worle man started showing his preserved body to English audiences in the early 1900s. Kap Dwa was then exhibited at various locations in Weston between 1914 and 1959, eventually moving to the USA.

Our forebears seem to have been fascinated by the unusual in nature and a dark-skinned, near-naked body, stretched out 12ft in its glass case certainly came in that category. The two heads lent some credence to early theories that this was some sort of mutation of twins but, whatever the explanation, those who paid twopence a time to see Kap Dwa doubtless felt their money well spent.

Joseph Sewell's shoes can be seen in the Somerset County Museum, at Taunton.

Windmills

'Farmers paid one shilling per coomb of 16 to 18 stones (and) in addition to the prices for grinding, the miller was allowed his grist, namely four pounds of meal from each coomb ground.'

The first mention of windmills in Somerset occurs early in the 13th century when examples are recorded at Seavington St Michael and on the northern slope of the Polden Hills at Woolavington. Others followed and by the early 14th century there was a significant number of such mills on private and monastic lands, especially on the higher ground areas adjoining the Somerset Levels. Except in periods of heavy rainfall rivers like the Parrett and the Brue flow only sluggishly and this may have prompted the construction of windmills in those places where water mills could not function.

Based on the evidence of early illustrations and carvings the first windmills were of the post mill type. For stability the main post was buried in the ground on a natural or artificial mound and provided with wooden supporting legs. The elevated and pivoted body of the mill was boarded in and gabled and four square sails were usual, along with a tail pole for turning the structure to catch the wind. By the time of the Black Death the main building period for these simple wooden post mills was over but, frequently rebuilt, many of them continued to grind corn for human use and pulses for animal feed for many years.

Unlike the experience in counties such as Norfolk, windmills played little part in the draining of Somerset's wetlands. They continued at work on the best of the early higher ground sites but from the early 18th century most were of the tower mill type, constructed in brick or stone - mainly blue lias - and using iron for strengthening purposes. Other improvements included the use of a revolving cap to replace the pivoting main body and the provision of luffing chains or a fantail to help turn the sails into the wind. These wooden sails, four in number, were mostly open lattice work, rectangular in shape and with a covering of canvas sailcloth unfurled when the mill was in action. In Somerset, tower mills were generally on the small side, around 25-30ft high and 12ft-15ft in diameter, but other features could differ considerably. Inside the mill the revolving upper millstone and static lower one would come from Draycott or Ham Hill, Wales, the Pennines, or even France. Their cutting, cleaning, positioning and feeding were all part of the miller's skills.

Some mills were worked by the same family for generations with occasional periods of high drama punctuating the normal pattern of milling life. Perhaps the most awesome moments occurred when the wind rose unexpectedly. If the miller had misjudged the weather the older mills, with only a simple wooden friction brake, could prove extremely difficult to control. Hair raising stories are told of wildly spinning sails, maximum effort on the smoking brake and even feeding every ounce of corn through the stones in an effort to slow the process down. If these efforts failed quite serious fires could result. Burnt Mill Field at Wedmore suggests its own story.

A windmill at Berrow was an early victim of high winds while a gale in 1898 blew the sails completely off the Heath House mill. Earlier in the century, the *Taunton Courier* had reported the dramatic end of the Shapwick windmill on 29 November 1836. William Jones and his brother ran a small farm and supplemented their income by working an old wooden stump mill there but in a gale on that fateful Tuesday they just could not control the wildly spinning vanes. Eventually the machinery got totally out of control and brought the entire mill down on top of them. William Jones lost his life in this incident which a subsequent inquest heard was by no means uncommon.

There was legislation precluding the building of windmills too near turnpike roads, and local animals generally got used to the sight and sound of a windmill. However, the sails of a mill at Weare on one occasion so frightened a passing horse that its rider was thrown to the ground and killed, the mill subsequently being closed down. At Watchfield a different horse story is told. It involved John Spearing, a senior member of a milling family, who bet a visiting Bristol racehorse owner £10 that his mixed ancestry workhorse would win a race between the two provided his master chose the course. Craftily John chose one around the mill and duly collected his winnings when the thoroughbred would go nowhere the creaking sails and inner rumblings.

Somerset is fortunate in that two windmills survive from a total that was once around one hundred. Stembridge Mill at High Ham is a National Trust property noted for its thatched cap while Ashton Windmill at Chapel Allerton is operated by a partnership between Sedgemoor District Council and local people. Along with the examples of windmill towers surviving after conversion to dwellings and other uses, and of former locations where a name like Windmill Hill denotes an old site, they help in recalling earlier ages when windmills were a common and valuable part of country life.

The restored Ashton Windmill is open to the public at certain times.

Past Pastimes

*'the person who breaks the most heads and saves
his own will be entitled to the prize'*

Games, contests and other pastimes have long been part of the British way of life. Dancing, singing, acting, board games, cards or dice featured in countless indoor pursuits, while outdoor fun ranged from athletic activity like throwing, vaulting and the various forms of fighting to examples of ball dexterity and to the use and abuse of other living creatures. The names of some of these early games are strange to us, like cambucan which seems to have been a form of golf, closh which was related to ninepins and 'ad pilam' where players had to hit a ball through a suspended loop.

Starting back in the 14th century playing games on holy days came under increasing attack from successive monarchs partly for religious reasons and partly because they needed bowmen for their warlike ambitions and feared that playing games would prove more attractive than archery practice. An Act of Parliament of 1542 stipulated fines for those fathers or masters who failed to provide 'for every man and child of from 7 to 17 a bow and two shafts to bring them up in shooting'. At the same time it restricted the playing of 'cards, bowls, closh, coyting and logating'. Other games were prohibited in other statutes with penalties ranging from 'a day in the stocks openly' to six days in prison for workmen who played 'unthrifty games'. James I offered a more sympathetic view in a Declaration made in May 1618 but authority returned to its oppressive ways in such periods of religious extremes as the years of Cromwell's Commonwealth.

Prior to James I declaring 'May-games, Whitson-ales and morris-daunces' to be 'harmless recreation' after church on Sundays and holy days the Chapter of Wells Cathedral had sternly warned its community of vicars against 'playing forbidden games, such as handball or the like' and threatened periods of suspension for any infringements 'because much scandal is caused to the Church'. Doubtless clerics were not the only offenders but shortly afterwards, in 1575, parson Nicholas Rogers of Priston was summoned for 'playing at an unlawful game called bowles.'

Traditional popular games, which included football and 'tenez', survived despite restrictions and, as the years passed, more liberal attitudes resulted in games becoming more varied and widespread. An example is the game of fives which became increasingly popular in Somerset from the 17th century. A sort of outdoor version of squash, this game was initially played against a wall of the local church tower. As it grew more popular incumbents at Williton, Wrington, Montacute, and Martock all had to urge their churchwardens to put a stop to the damage being caused. At Martock the vestry recorded 'much mischief' being done to the windows of the church and 'much wickedness causing swearing, quarrelling and fighting' when the game was being played in the churchyard.

The vicar at Montacute put a stop to his fives problems by having the base of the village cross dumped on the playing area, while the churchwardens of Martock paid out 3s 6d to have a ditch dug across theirs. Taking the hint the game then moved to various local village inns where a number of fives walls still survive. One such is at the Fleur-de-Lis at Stoke-sub-Hamdon where spectator takings once reached £60 when local star players John Palmer and Frederick Fame routed two rivals from Bath. In the process Palmer achieved a mighty hit which rebounded off the fives wall and rocketed back over the spectators onto the pub roof.

The fives walls in South Somerset were imposing and elegant stone structures as this former wall at South Petherton reveals.

In addition to horse riding and racing, ferrets, dogs, bulls, hawks and fighting cocks have all figured prominently in the list of Somerset pastimes which involved other living creatures. In 1768 the mastiffs of Somerset were said to be 'the boldest of all others' when it came to baiting bulls, bears and badgers. There were bull rings in several of the county's market towns where a bull or bear would be tethered from behind and cruelly baited by dogs who risked being kicked or gored. A baited bull was used on one occasion to overturn the table at which John Wesley was preaching in Pensford, and there are records of a

13

bull fight at Burnham-on- Sea where the successful rustic matador stood on top of the sad carcase waving a Union Jack to celebrate his victory.   The traditional day for bull torment was November 5th. At Axbridge on that day a church service attended by the mayor and corporation was followed by the release of a bull in the Square and its pursuit down Moorland Street by a crowd armed with staves and clubs. At Outing Batch the exhausted and terrified animal was tethered to the bull anchor and beaten to death. The 'cagman' then performed his rough butchery on the carcase to provide meat for the poor of the town.

Cock fighting took place all over Somerset, in locations as far apart as Yeovil, Wellington and Minehead. The Vicar of Minehead and the Squire of Dunster were noted for matching their gamecocks but the great event of the cock-fighting calendar took place at Ansford each Shrove Tuesday. Not only were the birds of Somerset there matched against the best from Wiltshire and Dorset but the spectators were also provided with free pea soup and bacon. Bristol's five cockpits regularly hosted inter-county events and 3-day 'local derbys' were held at the White Lion in Bath in 1724 and 1736.

The name 'Cockspurs' supports the belief that this house once had a cockpit in the roof space. Others were adjacent to public houses but then moved out to remote country areas when public feeling turned against the activity.

The inter-county and other major contests usually featured 30 to 50 cocks a side, involved a day for weighing and two for fighting and offered up to five guineas for each battle won with a main prize of a hundred guineas. To prevent interference with the birds each contest often had official feeders but the one at Somerton in 1761 stipulated 'Each gentleman to feed his own Cocks.' A mid-afternoon dinner was provided at some events and entrance to the pits cost around five shillings. An affair at Hinton Charterhouse in 1758 was promoted as a 'Battle Royal' and included a prize of 'a gold laced hat'. The same event stipulated that 'the dead cocks and those that ran away' were to belong to the host landlord. Such cock fighting contests were popular for much of the 18th century but were finally outlawed by the passing of the Cruelty of Animals Act in 1849.

In the 16th century cock-throwing was one of the regular Shrove Tuesday entertainments, along with climbing a greasy pole for a leg of mutton, chasing a pig with a soaped tail or watching women race and box. Cocks, the farmyard variety rather than the valuable fighting birds, also featured in an activity known as 'cock-squailing' in which the participants paid to throw a stick at a tethered bird. The thrower who knocked the bird down could keep it if he reached the poor creature before it had regained its feet. The practice was eventually banned and clay cocks used instead.

Some activities were linked with specific parts of the county like the great miners' quoits contests of the North Somerset coalfield which involved throwing a 8-12lb iron quoit at a stake 18 yards away. Somerset also contributed to the 'Bristol School' of pugilists with several of its sons becoming local or national champions, among them George Millsom, one of a sizeable Bath contingent, and Taunton carpenter Tom Gaynor who beat Charles Gybletts in 1828 in a tremendous 51-round contest. Taunton also staged wrestling contests between local men and wrestlers from Devon, but the use of hobnail boots made them very different from today's version of the sport.

The church porch at Stratton-on-the-Fosse used to host various quiet games of marbles but at places like Wiveliscombe, Wedmore and Worle large crowds were attracted to the more dramatic back-sword and cudgel bouts in which drawing blood by a blow to your opponent's head was necessary to secure victory. These were often staged on a raised platform and the usual weapon was a 2ft stick with a knob at one end and a wicker guard at the other. The only defence was a strap which was formed into a triangle from leg to wrist via the raised elbow. Things could get rather bloody, especially if the 'sticklers' who acted as seconds got drawn in, making the prize mentioned in the opening quotation very well deserved. Wincanton, apparently, hosted Somerset v All England contests in 1785 and around 1790.

Today's pastimes may be more organised, regulated and civilised but, clearly, our ancestors did manage to enjoy themselves in one way or another. Quite how they achieved this when playing 'half-bowles', which used something akin to a conventional wood cut in half, is not clear!

LITTLE JACK HORNER: Thomas or John?

Little Jack Horner
Sat in a corner,
Eating his Christmas pie.
He put in his thumb
And pulled out a plum,
And said, "What a good boy am I!".

There have been many accounts, told or recorded, as to the origins of this 'nursery' rhyme. One of the most persistent stories involves John Horner who, it was alleged, stole the deeds to the Manor of Mells from the Abbot of Glastonbury, just prior to the dissolution of the abbey in the 16th century. Although it is known that John Horner, in fact, purchased the manor following the dissolution, the association of this transaction with underhand methods has not dimmed over 460 years. It is certain that the dissolution of Glastonbury Abbey was traumatic in the short and long term to the local and wider community; it also appears that the Horner family attracted much hostility during the time of this upheaval. With the passage of time and partly as a result of the 'nursery' rhyme it has been assumed that John Horner was the villain of the piece; but was he?

There have been disputes as to whether or not the nursery rhyme referred to an ancestor of the Horner family. It has been suggested, for example, that it can be traced to 1767 when the rhyme appeared in a popular comical story in verse *The History of Jack Horner*. There are, however, earlier references, and it is likely that the rhyme has a long history, being included in stories and ballads because of its popularity and its allusion to opportunism. *The Oxford Dictionary of Nursery Rhymes* merely says... *'from the historical angle, there is no objection to the short rhyme having originally referred to the Horner ancestor.'*

Thomas Horner, a steward to Abbot Richard Whyting of Glastonbury Abbey, purchased several manors in Somerset following the confiscation of the abbey holdings by Henry VIII. *The Oxford Dictionary of Nursery Rhymes* continues...

'Glastonbury, at the beginning of 1539, was the only religious house in Somerset left untouched, and it was the richest abbey in the Kingdom. When Abbot Whyting was on trial for his life, Thomas Horner was a member of the complaisant jury which condemned him. It is admitted that Horner benefited by being a King's man, and the local people may well have had their own ideas about how he acquired his estates. A couplet, still current in Somersetshire, which was put on record as early as 1680 runs....

Hopton, Horner, Smyth, Thynne,
When abbots went out, they came in'.

Abbot Whyting was dragged on a hurdle to the summit of Glastonbury Tor, and there executed. The aged abbot had a reputation as a saintly man and one can imagine the feelings of local people and others at this crime, one of the most ruthless and unnecessary acts ever sanctioned by Henry VIII.

Another member of the Horner family, John of Cloford, took up residence in Mells, and so began the long association of his descendants with the area.

It is tempting to link John Horner with the Jack Horner of the nursery rhyme, Jack often being substituted for John. However, it is more likely that the rhyme refers to the bachelor Thomas Horner, a member of the jury disposed to comply with the King's wishes, with tragic results.

If the nursery rhyme does refer to Thomas Horner, why Jack? This could have been a deliberate change of name by the author, Jack being another word for knave. 'Jack the Lad' is still in current use to describe someone with an eye to the main chance.

The nursery rhyme could very well have come about as a safe, effective way of making people's feelings of outrage known at the time. After all we know that ballads were often used as a medium of protest when other channels were closed or forbidden.

The fact that Thomas Horner served on the jury that condemned Richard Whyting, and became the lord of several manors following the Crown seizure of church lands, could have led to understandable suspicions that he was favoured in their purchase, hence, possibly, the nursery rhyme. We may never know.

The Show At The End Of The Pier

During the hayday of paddle steamer excursions trips the Birnbeck Island pier
at Weston-super-Mare was the busiest in the Bristol Channel.

By the late 1940s the White Funnel fleet of paddle steamers that had returned from war service had been refurbished and augmented by two new paddlers the *Bristol Queen* (1946) and the *Cardiff Queen* (1947) built as reparation for vessels lost to P&A Campbell in the conflict.

We were not to know it then but the 1950s was the last great scene for excursion vessels in the Bristol Channel before the car and cheap foreign holidays drew the curtain on a century of day tripping between South Wales and the West Country. If you were not on board one of Campbell's steamers one of the best places to observe the movements of the fleet was from Prince Consort Gardens above Birnbeck Island at Weston-super-Mare.

The *Ravenswood* (1819), the oldest paddler in the fleet and the first Campbell's steamer to be built for the Bristol Channel service, plied mainly between Newport and Weston operating like a ferry on nearly all states of the tide. The *Glen Usk* (1914) would be back and forth from Weston to Cardiff, Barry Island, and Penarth. The *Glen Gower* (1922) would also call from time to time but was usually based in Swansea. The *Cardiff Queen* was based in Cardiff and did the long distance trips from South Wales. The *Britannia* (1896) and the *Bristol Queen* being larger and faster than the smaller members of the fleet did the 'down channel' trips from Bristol Hotwell pier to Ilfracombe and Lundy, a journey of 194 nautical miles in a day! Both of these ships would also call at Weston to embark and disembark passengers and this could mean four or five paddlers off the pier with all the captains eager to make a quick turn around.

Birnbeck Pier was the most difficult of all the piers in the Bristol Channel to call at. The tide set made mooring difficult at any state of ebb or flow and even the most experienced captains sometimes got it wrong. With a blustery wind the job was even more difficult and could get very exciting, if not nerve wracking, for passengers, onlookers and especially the bridge officers as several steamers manoeuvred in close proximity trying to get along-side the pier when shown the appropriate signal by the pier master.

The 'Cardiff Queen' at speed in the Bristol Channel.

Streams of Welsh day trippers would surge down the pier to Anchor Head and the esplanade to swell the crowds that would have arrived mainly by excursion train and charabancs to enjoy the delights of the Marine Lake, the donkey rides on the sands, the new swimming pool or the more sedate Winter Gardens. If it rained or the tide was out (the sea retreats a long way at Weston) the Grand Pier was a must with its rides, amuse-ments, candy floss, 'Kiss-me Quick' hats and all the razzmatazz of a day by the sea.

By late afternoon a steady stream of trippers would make their way back to the pier, families proceeding dads who were having a last pint before facing the ocean. As time drew on the steamer at the pier would hoot incessantly to hurry along the late comers, mothers herding children who kept running back to pick up dropped items like sandals, buckets and spades and wet bathing costumes. Mothers were also anxiously looking over their shoulders to see if father had at last made the pier.

Captains on the steamers off the pier waiting their turn and concerned about time and tide would also hoot impatiently, increasing the cacophony of ship's sirens. Eventually the last stragglers, nearly always the dads, noticeably suffering 'sea legs' even before they got to the gang plank, would be scolded aboard by both crew and wives to the relief of the fret-ting children. Not all trippers would make it before the last departure and some would arrive to see the *Glen Usk* or *Ravenswood* well on their way to the Welsh Coast.

One regular tripper only just made it aboard the steamer from a waterside bar and it was some little time before he recollected that he had agreed to stay overnight in Weston with his wife. What she had to say about this as she contemplated alone in her bed and break-fast accommodation can only be conjectured.

The Royal Forests

'the notorious asylum of a desperate clan of banditti
whose depredations were a terror to the surrounding parishes'

The Rev. John Collinson, writing in 1791, was referring to the reputation held by Longleat Wood earlier in the 18th century. The wood, located just south of Frome, was one of the last surviving parts of the ancient Selwood Forest which straddled Somerset's border with Wiltshire and was one of five major royal forests which were once an important feature of the county.

Although royal visits were rare, substantial areas of Somerset were once part of the Crown's forest lands. The main royal forest areas in addition to Selwood were those of Mendip, Exmoor, North Petherton and Neroche (south east of Taunton), and there was another boundary forest in the Keynsham-Kingswood area of which Collinson recorded 'a great part of this district was anciently a royal chace.' While forests originally belonged to the Crown, a noble might be permitted to own a chace, of which there was another example near Axbridge. Additionally, the Quantocks embraced a forest of some sort while the area around Somerton seems to have been a warren which functioned as a forest but with hares the protected animals instead of the more usual deer population.

In contrast with today's perception of a forest, the royal forests of the past were not always heavily wooded. As on much of Exmoor today, they were more likely to embrace large tracts of scrubland and open moor. This in turn provides one of the clues to the origins of the royal forests as the land which was not claimed for early settlement or pasture tended to become the home territory for the wild animals which provided food and sport for a succession of warrior/hunter kings and their chief nobles. To protect these privileges and their opportunities for profit such areas became increasingly subject to the royal prerogative, although not necessarily to royal ownership.

The practice of hunting deer and wild boar was quite widespread well before the Norman Conquest but became formalised during the Norman dynasty. Starting with William I, the Norman kings extended and defined the forests and provided stringent laws for their control. Irrespective of ownership of the land, the King had absolute title to the deer population as well as control over the timber and a very useful entitlement to the fines and other revenues.

Successive later monarchs also made their mark on the forest scene. In his 1184 Assize of Woodstock Henry II defined all his royal forests and laid down a code for their control with courts, justices and sanctions against offenders. At that period anyone killing a royal animal might expect severe treatment. Indeed the Chief Justice to Richard I warned of the end to a trend towards leniency and a return to the laws of the first royal Henry when anyone convicted could expect 'to lose his eyes and his virility'. Hanging was also on the cards and even innocent dogs in forest areas could expect to be 'expeditated' and have 'cut away the balls of their forefeet' to render them incapable of molesting game.

King John, with legendary greed, claimed large increases in forest land but was forced into a disafforestation period by the Magna Carta revolt. Edward I tried the same trick but with no more success. From a peak of around 140 the number of royal forests then began to decline, a process accelerated by the Stuart kings who sold many off to meet their constant need for funds. A statute in the reign of Charles I enacted that no forest existed where a forest court had not been held for 60 years.

This 12th century defensive mound survives within the 72 hectares of Neroche Forest.

To govern the forests there was a pyramid hierarchy topped by a Warden or Keeper of the Forest, usually a person of high rank. His control was exercised through verderers and foresters. The latter were the equivalent of gamekeepers but the former were given wide powers to protect the vert (wood, pasture etc) and venison, especially against poaching and trespass. Usually four for each forest, the verderers were elected for life by freeholders of the county and exercised their powers through a Court of Attachment which met every 40 days. Another court met twice a year to deal with rights and privileges but all major issues were heard before the King's visiting Justices of Eyre who dealt with cases referred by the verderers, kept a watchful eye on royal interests and undertook a certain amount of county administration.

The royal forests had traditionally embraced some grazing land and, as the population grew, the royal wardens found it increasingly profitable to let out areas for the summer pasturing of cattle, sheep and horses. Rates and records were the province of the agisters who sometimes published their prices at the local markets, as they did on Exmoor.

Another forest officer, the regarder, had the job of preventing forest encroachment and undertook regular surveys to ensure boundaries were not infringed.

Those who lived in the forest were something of a community apart. Such forest dwellers normally paid their tithes to the Crown and might thus find themselves excluded from the parish system and the support it provided in times of adversity. Indeed, in some parts of the country unmarried mothers-to-be were sent to homes in the forest for their confinement as a way of avoiding them becoming a charge on the parish. Since it was also difficult to apply normal parish law in the wilder and more remote forest areas they were sometimes the refuge of vagrants, fugitives and villains of various sorts. Collinson mentioned the coining of money taking place in Selwood Forest while Kingswood Forest was, at one period, well-known for its footpads and other disaffected inhabitants

Perhaps the most notable of the Somerset forests was the Royal Forest of Mendip. At its heart was Cheddar, originally owned by the Saxon kings of Wessex, and the site of a royal palace and later of royal hunting lodges. At its zenith the Mendip forest extended from the mouth of the River Axe at Uphill to the Selwood Forest boundary at Frome and provided huge quantities of venison for the tables of the monarch and his favourites. Its timber was in demand for building, scaffolding and smelting fuel and provided further funds for the Crown, while fines for trespass and poaching also went to the King. Surprisingly, local clergy and other men of the cloth featured among those who had to pay up for indulging in such clandestine activities.

King John, perennially short of money, sold the manor of Cheddar to the Bishop of Wells, where the town's wards became known as verderies. The sale related mainly to land ownership and for many years there was frequent conflict between the church and the lingering royal administration. Boundary restrictions followed in subsequent reigns with the eventual end of Mendip Forest coming in 1338. In other parts of the county royal rights were increasingly translated into licences for local landowners, usually in return for a fee or favour, and over the years the forests became less royal and more like private parks. Their licensèd owners treated the deer as their own and by the 16th century many were keeping packs of hounds to facilitate their hunting.

The decline of the royal forests which began in the 14th century was hastened by the Parliamentary victory in the Civil War and then by the later years of land enclosure. Some survived to pass into the hands of the Forestry Commission when it was established in 1919 or to become National Parks but most of the original Somerset forest areas have largely disappeared. Fortunately Exmoor remains to convey an idea of what the open type of royal forest used to be like but of the denser woodland category only small patches survive at places like Kings Wood near Wrington and Cheddar Wood near Shipham. Happily, the Somerset woods of the Forestry Commission, now managed by its Forest Enterprise Agency are in good hands and examples like the Neroche site in the Blackdown Hills not only provide total woodland care but also the preservation of the ancient defensive site there.

Market Houses

'It consists on the ground floor of a pitched market house for corn and cheese, with shambles behind for meat, bacon etc. Over the main building is a mezzanine floor, forming an extensive floor for corn and by its side a spacious and well lighted reading room.'

These three illustrations give some idea of the variety to be found among Somerset's market houses. The one above is at Clevedon and those below at Castle Cary (left) and Burnham-on-Sea (right). The opening lines are from an 1855 newspaper description of the Castle Cary market house.

Markets themselves date back to Saxon times and for hundreds of years were essential to local trading of all kinds They grew steadily in number and size and by the 17th century had frequently become chaotic, despite the various officials and regulations designed to control their conduct.

Taunton's produce and livestock markets were originally held on the same spot and might have as many as a hundred butchers slaughtering and selling meat from the traditional shambles stalls.

Other traders of every sort and size also competed for space and custom. The event brought in tinkers, hucksters, mountebanks and preachers. Local village folk tried to earn a little extra by selling their produce and a huge crowd attended seeking supplies, a bargain or just some lively and colourful entertainment.

Add on the tethered animals, dozens of dogs and an increasing carpet of refuse and it is little wonder that a 1768 Act of Parliament authorising a market house and new

arrangements, said of the existing Taunton market that 'removing the same would be of great convenience to the inhabitants'.

In other Somerset towns also the provision of a market house became part of the move to make markets tidier and more organised. They were used to store goods and equipment, provide facilities for trading or discussing trade and, in some cases, provided such extras as an assembly room, music gallery or even lock-up cells. Quite a few market houses were built in the 19th century and most were quite fine buildings.

Although their uses changed with the times at least sixteen market houses survive in the county and still serve its communities in one way or another.

Pictured here are the former market houses at Radstock (top right), Taunton (centre) and Martock (bottom right) and those at Minehead (top left), Crewkerne (centre) and Wells (bottom left).

Albert Day, the Mark Iron Founder

*Among the nettles and wild flowers in the corner of the
car park at 'The Barn' Nailsea was the remains of an old cider mill.
The eye was drawn to the fine cast iron moulding on the top of the frame,*
A. DAY. MARK

Photo Roy Gallop

Albert Day set up a foundry in East Mark in about 1839. The village is on the Somerset Levels and lies between Wedmore and Burnham-on-Sea. He started a smithy and installed a cupola for smelting iron; the site was well developed by 1886 with cottages for the workers. The foundry produced cider presses, apple mills, cheese presses, railings, sign posts, farm machinery and many other iron implements which were sold extensively in Somerset and also in other parts of England and South Wales.

When Albert died in 1893 aged 81 years the firm continued to trade, run by his two sons John and George. John died in1929 and a syndicate of local farmers bought the factory which was managed by a local agricultural engineer, Bert Wensley, until 1950.

The Days were staunch Methodists and their substantial and long lasting iron grave memorials can be seen at the Methodist graveyard (right) at East Mark. The gates of the Parish Church (above), Mark (1848) are a fine example of the Day foundry skills.

There are still many items of their work to be discovered, especially railings and gates in graveyards and farm machinery in neglected corners of farmyards. The Day cheese press in the reception area of the Somerset Rural Life Museum in Glastonbury has a fine casting of a rural scene. Cider presses and mills occur occasionally in pub gardens. Look out for the founder's trademark.

Fortune my Foe

***"I Desire all good Christians to take warning
this Day by my untimely End."***

So began the dying confession of Jack White, a Wincanton man who was hanged for murder at crossroads near Bratton Seymour on 19 August 1730. He was paying the penalty for a savage attack on one Bob Sutton in which he apparently grabbed a stake from the hedgerow, 'beat out one of his eyes, ran the stick in at his mouth and out through the neck, and otherwise mangled his victim.' As was the custom of the time crowds of local people turned up to witness White's unhappy fate at the very spot where his dreadful crime had been committed.

The broadsheet account of Jack White's final words continues:-

"I was born in Wincanton, of honest and industrious Parents, and lived honestly and soberly until the 26th Year of my Age, when I married in an honest Family, and liv'd lovingly with my Wife. Nor was I ever maliciously inclined to hurt Man, Woman or Child, till the Time that this unfortunate Accident happen'd, which that Day I little thought of: but going along Wincanton, one Gilbert, at the Sign of the Sun, called me into his House, where I drank hard; when the Deceased came in, who was in Liquor, and offered me Drink to go along with him, which I agreed to, and went with him out of Town, directing him in his Way, as well as I was able; but being overcome with Liquor, I laid down to sleep, whilst the Deceased went forwards; who missing his way came back to me again and waked me, and begg'd of me to go a little further with him. I agreed, and in our Way we met two Women, one of whom I saluted, but the other being stubborn, provoked me to strike her, and as far as my Memory can retain, the Deceased and I had Words about them, and also would force me to go along with him to his Journey's End; taking a Counter out of his Pocket, cursing and swearing that it was half a Guinea, and that he would spend it all upon me. We went on till we came to that fatal Place, where through Drunkenness, and the Devil's Suggestion, I embrew'd my Hands in his innocent Blood, for which I beg heartily the Forgiveness of God. I die in Peace with all Mankind, imploring the prayers of all good Christians, and commend my soul to the Mercy of Jesus Christ, on whom I wholly rely for salvation.'

Death by hanging had been part of the British system of 'justice' for centuries at the time of Jack White's death. In the feudal years some high nobles and churchmen had the right to hang those who offended and even when punishment became more regularised hanging remained the ultimate deterrent, not only for murder and other serious violence but also in any case where goods worth more than a shilling were stolen. A rise in serious crime in the second half of the 16th century led to an increase in hangings and to London getting its first permanent gallows in 1571. Located at Tyburn, these had 18ft high cross beams which could accommodate eight victims at a time.

Carrying out executions in public was considered important in conveying a strong message of discouragement against law breaking. This was particularly the case after the Monmouth rebellion when so many Somerset men paid dearly for their involvement at prominent locations throughout the county. They are still remembered at places like Heddon Oak near Stogumber and Gallows Oak just south of Chard. County maps and local lore also remember other execution sites at Felon's Oak on the road south from Lower Rodhuish, Gibbet Hill on the Nunney side of Frome, Execution Field at Kenn, Hanging Wood west of Butcombe and Gibbets Brow near Compton Martin. To afford watchers a good view prominent places were always chosen, like the spot at Shute Shelve Hill where a group of Worle men hanged for a murder conspiracy prompted the parish register comment 'a good president (sic) for wicked people.'

Capital offences continued to increase from the middle of the 17th century with most Somerset executions taking place at Ilchester, first in Gallows Five Acre just half a mile along the Yeovil Road and then at the county gaol after 1811. Gallows were in use at Stone near Taunton by 1792 and continued their sombre work until 1810. Ilchester finally relinquished its grisly responsibility on 1 March 1843 when Wilton took over as the county gaol. After forty years the mantle then passed to Shepton Mallet prison which witnessed its first execution on 13 March 1889. From 1868 such events had no longer been public occasions and the macabre 'celebrations' which attended them had finally come to an end.

Burglary and horse or sheep stealing predominated among capital crimes with quite a few murders and highway robberies and occasionally something different such as forgery or returning early after transportation. Some cases seem especially poignant like that of poor 29-year old Joan Tottle who was hanged on Stone Gallows in 1793 for 'the murder of her bastard child'. Two men from Bitton died together at Ilchester on 7 August 1799 for horse stealing after a Wiveliscombe man had paid the same penalty earlier in the year for stealing a piece of cloth. An 1816 hanging was for the rape of 6 year old Kezia Gould while three of the five men hanged together in 1817 had been convicted of burglary, one of them for stealing 96 watches from a Bridgwater jeweller. His defence was that he found them in a hayrick!

Perhaps the most dramatic event in the sad annals of Somerset hangings is the death of nine men on Stone Gallows on 15 April 1801. Two, or possibly three, of them had been caught up in the widespread food riots that followed the bad harvest of 1799 and had broken into a baker's premises in Old Cleeve, stolen bread and put the baker's wife in 'bodily fear'. The judge would take no account of the fact that they had left a token payment for the thirty loaves they had taken and sternly ruled that:-

'They had formed part of one of those mobs who, under pretence of lowering the price of provisions, committed depredations upon the community. It was, therefore, necessary, that such offences should receive from justice the utmost punishment that the law could inflict.'

The ages of men hanged in Somerset ranged from 18 to the late 50s. They suffered greatly from the moment of their conviction, those under sentence of death for murder having a particularly hard time. Immediately following the court appearance they were confined in their cells, 'fed with bread and water only' and allowed no visitors. In Taunton and Shepton Mallet gaols after 1866 they were further isolated by being 'clothed in a yellow dress.' A minister of religion paid a daily visit to offer spiritual support and exhortation to repentance.

Photo Roy Gallop

John Walford paid for his crime of passion at this quiet, wooded spot.

Executions generally took place on either a Monday or a Wednesday, usually in April but sometimes in August or September. The condemned prisoner had to rise early, 4am in the case of the three hanged at Kenn in 1830 for they had a long, slow journey to make in the Ilchester prison van. The nine who met their end at Stone in 1801 had to ride there in an open cart, sitting on the coffins that had been made in the prison workshops and escorted by mounted dragoons. Their ordeal was made worse by the huge crowds such events attracted and by the way the occasion was treated as festive, especially by insensitive and unruly elements. The hangings outside Ilchester gaol were watched from the bridge over the River Yeo or from prime spots along the banks for which the owners might charge anything up to a shilling. Soldiers attended the hangings at Stone and Kenn to prevent any disorder and when four men were hanged on the 30ft drop of Bristol's New Gaol after the 1831 riots artillery was brought along as well. Ten years earlier John Horwood had been the first man to die there after killing his sweetheart with a stone and achieved a macabre immortality when the surgeon who received his body for dissection had the skin tanned and used to cover a book recording the events of the trial and execution.

On the gallows the victim would be allowed time with the chaplain and given the opportunity to express remorse and regret. Many 'died to all appearances in a state of true penitence' but only the final removal of the supporting cart or trap and the last pitiful struggles of the swaying body made any impact on the rowdier elements in the crowd. Death was quick but the corpse was usually left hanging for about an hour before being taken to the mortuary for an inquest and then surrounded by quicklime and buried in the prison grounds or handed over to the surgeons for the benefit of medical science. An 'energetic address' from the officiating minister was usually the final on site event of the drama as the watchers drifted away to reflect on the morality of what they had seen or to wash away the haunting spectacle in further drinking.

John Walford's Gibbet, at the other end of Somerset to the site of Jack White's sorry story, has also been invested by its chroniclers with great poignancy. Located just off the A39 beyond Nether Stowey, it still appears on maps to mark the spot where John Walford was hanged in 1789 for the murder of his wife, a tragic end for a local lad to whom love had not been kind.

Dead Woman's Ditch where John Walford is said to have buried his murdered wife.

John, who worked as a charcoal burner in the hills between Nether Stowey and Crowcombe, had fallen in love with Ann Rich, the miller's daughter. However, her family would not let them wed and John fell an easy victim to the solace offered by Jane Thorney, the daughter of a fellow charcoal worker. An unwanted pregnancy and a loveless marriage led quickly to bitterness and acrimony. Within three weeks an evening of drinking and quarrelling culminated in trasgedy. Late home, Jane then wanted a reluctant John to take her drinking at the Castle of Comfort Inn. On the way an argument got out of hand and John grabbed a hedegrow stake and beat his nagging wife into permanent silence. He tried to conceal the body but Johns behaviour gave away his awful guilt and led to a confession.

After a short trial at Bridgwater John Walford was condemned to hang at the scene of his crime, an ironically beautiful spot looking out from the foothills and over the fields to Bridgwater Bay. A large and noisy crowd watched as he was brought to the spot by horse and cart and then permitted a few tender moments with Ann, his first love. All too soon she was pulled away, the noose placed around John's neck and the cart drawn forward to send the body jerking and swinging into space. In a final indignity it was cut down and suspended in a cage until the elements finally brought the whole grisly spectacle crashing back to earth and the whitened bones could be interred near the spot. Here, as at the other execution sites in Somerset, a quiet peace has now displaced the echoes of past horror.

Above are the opening bars of the melody, 'Fortune my Foe'. It was played so often at public executions that it became known as 'The Hanging Tune'.

Grave Concerns

Executed felons and those who took their own lives could expect little in the way of memorial, just burial beneath the gallows, in a prison graveyard or somewhere similarly unmarked, unconsecrated and uncelebrated. For others in the days before cremation became acceptable their grave site and grave furniture was directly related to wealth, status in the community and other such factors. As a onetime tombstone in Yatton church put it:

> *Here I lies behind the door.*
> *Here I lies because I'm poor.*
> *The further in the more you pay.*
> *But I lies here as well as they.*

A wealth of other sentiments and gems of wisdom have appeared on Somerset graves at various times. Some have a plaintive note, like the headstone in Wedmore's parish church which complains 'In health I left my home, my friends in joy to meet. It was Jesus met me on the way; I fell beneath his feet'. Joseph Horsey's altar tomb at Kingsbury was more matter-of-fact in recording his life as 'Seventy-two then stopt', adding 'yielding to death His vital breath into the grave he dropt.' An ailing 84-year old from the Bridgwater area suffered from 'a churchyard cough' until 'There came a wind north east and blew her off.'

WILLIAM BARNES: The Somerset Connection

William Barnes (1801-1886) was a schoolmaster, priest and poet. He was a gifted man of great scholarship and sensitivity. Although better known for his poems in the Dorset dialect, the place of his birth, he also pursued the craft of engraving in wood and copper. Very many fine examples of his work still exist today.

William attended a Church of England endowed school in Sturminster Newton, leaving when he was thirteen years old. He took up employment locally, working as a clerk in the office of Thomas Henry Dashwood, a solicitor. It was said that William secured this position on account of his superb handwriting and drawing skills. His ambition was to become an artist. On moving to Dorchester in 1818 to work for another solicitor, Thomas Coombes, he endeavoured to improve his skills as a wood and copper engraver, an interest he had acquired during schooldays. However, his desire to become a professional artist and engraver remained an unfulfilled ambition. Later family commitments made economic considerations a priority and he was unable to receive the training to refine his natural ability and skills. William's raw talent must have been recognised as over the years he accepted a fair number of engraving commissions. This not only gave him an opportunity to practise his craft but provided his family with much needed additional income.

It is likely that William's connections with Somerset began in 1825. In that year his future wife Julia and her family moved from Dorchester to Nailsea and it was there that William and Julia were married in the parish church of the Holy Nativity in 1827. Julia accompanied William to Mere in Wiltshire where he had been a schoolmaster since 1823. She was to play a vital role in the management of the school, a mixed establishment of boarders. In 1835 the Barnes family left Mere to set up a day and boarding school in Dorchester.

During the 1820s and 1830s Somerset featured prominently in many of the engravings cut by William Barnes, some based on his own sketches. During the 1840s William continued engraving, illustrating text books he wrote for use in his school. Although it is likely that by this time he had given up all hope of becoming a professional artist it is evident that he still enjoyed working in this particular craft form. In 1854 William contracted rheumatic fever, a condition which severely restricted the use of his hands, a cruel blow for an artist.

William cut over two hundred engravings and a small number of his Somerset subjects are reproduced here. For those who would like to know more an excellent book of the Somerset engravings of William Barnes, written by Laurence Keen, was published by Somerset County Library Services in 1989. The book contains 73 Somerset engravings. Copies can be found in Somerset County reference and lending libraries.

Top: *Brean Down and Black Rock. The ferry house below the cliff can still be seen today.*

Middle left: *Ruins of Walton Old Church, near Clevedon, also known as Walton Castle.*

Middle right: *Glastonbury Tor, sculpture on St Michael's Tower. The engraving gives a clearer image of the subject which has subsequently suffered from weathering.*

Bottom: *Ancient Barn at Chelvey.*

The Last Dung Putt

*The mechanisation of farming was greatly accelerated during the 1939- 45
World War. The days of horse drawn farm implements were
nearly over.......*

It was probably the spring of 1946, it was definitely after the V E celebrations that my father was left a message to contact John Adams at his home in the Chalks, Chew Magna.

John was a very old man, or so he seemed to me aged nine. He walked with two sticks and lived in a house in the narrow road leading into the village. John was a carpenter/wheel-wright who, because of acute arthritis, was no longer working and had not been able to complete an order for a dung putt, (a tipping farm cart). During the war John had been unable to find anyone who could finish the job for him. As the village was gradually returning to some sort of normality and father was no longer spending what little spare time he had as an air raid warden John hoped that he could finish and deliver the job for him.

Father worked for a company that owned a sawmill at Ubley about five miles away. They made a lot of timber products and he was their head joiner. He had been apprenticed as a wheelwright and had made many farm carts. His last big four-wheeled waggon was for Farmer Lawrence at Fairseat Farm, Chew Magna. Sadly this was never pulled by horses, the shafts were removed and a trailer hitch was fitted and it was pulled by a Fordson tractor.

We visited the old workshop beside the River Chew at Tonbridge, just below the mill. Everything lay in thick dust and had been shut up for some years. The dung putt was more complete than my father had imagined, the body was almost finished but it needed wheels, tipping mechanism and shafts plus the fittings and a paint job. Although the workshop had most things needed to complete the job it was very old fashioned, cramped and even more untidy than father's workshop at Ubley. There the joiners would work up to their bums in shavings (the resinous smell was almost intoxicating) and would pinch out their Woodbine stubs and drop them into the inflammable debris on the floor without a second thought.

Jim Boyd, a good friend of my father and very friendly towards me, was the yard foreman and in charge of the timber cutting. I could not take my eyes off his hands whenever I was in his company for he hardly had a complete digit on either hand.

Work proceeded through the spring evenings and the occasional Saturday. Father turned the wheel hubs, or bosses as he called them, on the lathe using Witch Elm. He chopped the mortises for the spokes and the wheels were nearly complete. The shafts had been completed in ash and meanwhile another recruit was busy with the metalwork. Percy, father's brother-in-law, had been a blacksmith until drafted into the Douglas Motorcycle factory at Kingswood near Bristol where he worked making areoplane parts for the dura-

The advantage of the tipping dung putt was that one man could tip the heaviest load.

tion of the war. Percy had sold his business and after hostilities worked as a delivery driver for a local grocer. However, he still from his garden shed, produced beautiful gates and railings and was a great mender of broken metal items for neighbours.

My role in all this was 'gofer' and 'holder upper' and any other task I was felt capable of doing. The big day was getting near when the steel tyres that Percy had sweated over would be shrunk onto the wooden wheels to hold the whole wheel tightly together. Boys love fires and I was no exception. Coal or coke was laid around the steel tyre and with the aid of an acetylene torch the tyre was brought to a bright heat. At a moment decided by Percy, father and two other volunteers lifted the tyre horizontally with tongs until it was over the wooden wheel laid on its side. The heat from the tyre was intense but without incident it was dropped over the wheel and tapped into place. When Percy was satisfied all was well water to quench the steel and to stop excessive burning was watering- canned over the tyre and wheel. Bright red streaming faces peered out of the billowing steam; one done one to go; down with the watering can and on with the kettle.

I do not remember John Adams coming to see either the bonding of the wheels or the finishing of the dung putt, perhaps he was too ill. Father mixed his own paints, lead oxide, ochres, linseed oil and driers, another local skill no longer practised as no one now would have the time. Paint was never wasted, whatever was left over was poured into an old oil drum and later would be used as primer or undercoat. The dung putt was not finished in the bright colours of his other carts and waggons, just a couple of shades of grey and some parts left unpainted but varnished. The days of coloured carts were over, the putt was as dull as my school uniform. Where the dung putt went or how long it lasted I do not know.

Two friends (Cox and Palfrey) returning from their stint in the forces bought the yard and workshop and set up as builders and funeral directors. Father eventually went to work for them and had several apprentices. His last apprentice before he retired was Michael Rowe who now owns the business and continues trading there.

Collections of farm carts, waggons and agricultural machinery are not uncommon, but the dung putt, being a rather mundane and far from glamorous vehicle, is not so well represented. A good example can be seen at the Rural Life Museum, Glastonbury and an excellent recreation of a wheelwright's shop at the Radstock Museum.

Noyfull Fowles and Vermin

Extract from the Wedmore churchwardens' accounts 1824-5
'Paid for polecats, hedgehogs and sparrows, 5s 2d.'

In times of less sophisticated husbandry any wild creature which had a taste for crops or livestock represented a serious threat to the food supplies of a country community. By the time of Henry VIII the depredations of rooks, crows and choughs had become so serious that legislation had to be enacted in 1532-3 requiring each parish to provide a net for their capture. A further statute which followed in 1566 stipulated that all landowners should contribute to a fund from which to reward the destruction of what were colourfully described as 'Noyful Fowles and Vermin'. The level of payment was set at a penny for the heads of three adult crows or six young owls, with the same amount for six unbroken eggs.

For the next 300 years churchwardens' accounts in Somerset were to feature many such outpayments for the slaughter of predatory wildlife, frequently referring to the creatures by their local names. Minehead, Luccombe and Porlock all record sums paid out for 'fitchets', better known as polecats and once so numerous that 76 were killed in Wedmore in 1720. Some places recorded polecats as 'feeches' while others listed 'peimagettes' (magpies), 'wants' (moles) and 'whoops' (bull-finches).

The common birds all had a price on their heads along with rats, mice, stoats, foxes, martens, hedgehogs and the occasional otter. Rates varied over the years and from place to place, but with foxes fetching anything from a shilling at Axbridge to double that at Cheddar it is small wonder that those on a low income sought to earn a bit extra by their slaughter. With dogs, nets, traps, lures and later guns members of many a village family would set out to capture unwary predators and deliver their heads to the Parish Meeting or Vestry for the appropriate cash payment.

For larger birds Cheddar paid a shilling a dozen but would only hand over a penny for twelve sparrows compared with the twopence being offered by neighbouring Axbridge. By 1720 Wedmore's rate had reached threepence for each of the 230 dozen caught in that year and by 1837 Martock was paying sixpence a dozen for the 5,988 sparrows caught there.

An early sign that the whole process was getting a bit expensive appears in the Minehead accounts for 1751 which contained a minute declaring:-

'This Vestry do resolve that no future Churchwarden shall pay any of the parish's money for killing any foxes, badgers or other vermint or destructive birds.'

Traditional estates had long had their own exterminators - Nettlecombe Estate recording a payment of a guinea to Thomas Calloway for a year's molecatching in 1799 and the same sum for the services of a ratcatcher - and the enclosure process was now to hasten the rise of the professional gamekeeper who hung out the creatures he had trapped or shot in hideous but compelling rows. Most of the earlier 'vermin' statutes were repealed in 1863 as the shotgun took over and eventually even the time honoured scarecrow gave way to a more modern fate for the creatures once labelled 'Noyfull Fowles and Vermin'.

Porlock Pound

Wild creatures were not the only ones who posed a threat to precious crops and garden produce. Stray sheep, goats and cattle could also cause havoc and, in the centuries before modern fencing, frequently did so. In manorial times such local strays were the responsibility of the pinder who had to round them up and place them in the pinfold until the owner could be contacted. In the form of the village pound this practice lingered on well into the last century. A few pounds have survived in Somerset and several streets named Pound Lane mark the former location of others.

The simplest pounds usually consisted of a small square patch of ground surrounded by a low wall of stone. Hatch Beauchamp had an octagonal one and at least one Somerset example had a high wall with viewing slits that could be used from horseback. At Somerton getting an animal released involved a settlement for any damage it had done and then a 4d 'turnkey' payment to the hayward. Various old manorial court records contain details of fines imposed on the owners of strays and, sometimes, of disputes that arose from their straying.

The Turnpike Trusts

'The new line of turnpike road.......has opened a new and convenient communication across a district heretofore impassable.'

For some 150 years of the 18th and 19th centuries the only prospect of achieving any degree of comfort when travelling by road in Somerset lay in using a route maintained by one of the county's turnpike trusts. Usually local enterprises, these trusts were authorised by statute to raise capital for road improvements and then to service the loans by collecting tolls from the road users at specified locations. Apart from soldiers, mailcoaches and a few local exceptions such as farmers and churchgoers, all vehicles, animals and foot passengers had to stop at the 'pikes' or tollgates and pay the appropriate amount shown on the tollboard before they could proceed. There were, of course, a few hardy and wily travellers who preferred a furtive trip across the fields to avoid payment, the distributors of North Somerset coal being notable among these.

The former Muchelney tollhouse of the Langport, Somerton & Castle Cary Trust. The bay for collecting tolls is clearly visible on the front of this tiny, but attractive, building.

Shelter was usually provided for those manning the tollgates and a number of the permanent tollhouses have survived. Their design and size - anything from a tiny hut or cottage to a 2-storey stone building - tended to vary with the importance of the gate and from trust to trust, but most had a protruding bay to help spot approaching traffic and make sure a toll was collected from it. The gatekeepers themselves were originally trust employees but so many failed to hand over all their takings that auctioning the collecting rights annually became standard practice after 1773. Bidding against an hour glass was common and many bidders were farmers or innkeepers. It was not unknown for the worth of a gate to be overstated, for trust nominees to try to push up the bidding or for potential bidders to agree not to bid against one another!

The first turnpike trust to be established in Somerset was the Bath Trust which started life in 1707, the Bristol Trust following in 1727 and the Bridgwater Trust in 1730. Resentment against the gates and tolls was particularly marked around Bristol but eventually subsided, just as the initial poor surfaces improved under the influence of men like John Loudon Macadam and his grandson. The last Somerset trust was the Wells, Highbridge & Cheddar which obtained authority for its single route in 1841, no doubt influenced by the general increase in road activity which had begun around 1805. However 1841 was also the year in which the infant railway system reached Somerset and turnpike revenues soon declined rapidly, adding to previous Parliamentary anxiety about the extent of turnpike debt. After legis-

This surviving tollgate once belonged to the Wells Trust. Its height was designed to prevent horsemen jumping it to avoid paying the toll.

lation in 1862 the individual trusts began to be wound up, particularly in the 1870s, and their road maintenance responsibilities were taken over by the new local highway boards.

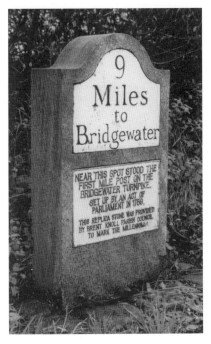

Until 1759 the turnpike road north from Bridgwater only extended as far as Puriton, the link on to Bristol being completed in that year.

The number of turnpike trusts and the profile of their roads rarely remained static for long but immediately before the advent of the railways a total of 23 Somerset turnpike trusts controlled 904 miles of road. The mileage of 13 of these trusts exceeded 40m with the largest being Langport (80.8m), Taunton (75m) and Wiveliscombe (63.8m). However only 9 of the 23 could be considered financially sound and the trust system was clearly in no position to meet the new threat which the trains represented. In 1846 the trusts taking the most in tolls were Bath (£8205), Taunton (£5020), Bristol (£4204), Shepton Mallet (£3553) and Frome (£3417). Others with significant earnings were the Black Dog, Bridgwater, Bruton, Chard, Crewkerne and Ilminster, the Langport, Somerton & Castle Cary, the Minehead United, Radstock, Wells, Wincanton and Yeovil trusts. Those taking less than £1000 were the High Ham & Ashcott, Ilchester, Martock & South Petherton, Wedmore, West Harptree & Chew Magna and Weston-super-Mare & Worle trusts, the latter collecting only £70 . 17s . 5d.

Happily we still have some reminders of the turnpike age with quite a few tollhouses and milestones surviving, along with a tollgate at Street and many smaller items in the county's museums.

Street Streams
"Dear Gutter of Stowey"

One way or another most Somerset towns owe their location and development, at least partially, to water. Vital for both human and animal existence it also had a further influence in terms of providing power and transport. A happy reminder of this link survives in several towns in the county where streams still run along or beside working thoroughfares, significantly enhancing their interest and attractiveness.

A prime example is the cathedral city of Wells. One of the many benefits bestowed upon it by the mid-15th century incumbency of Bishop Bekynton was a supply of water from St Andrew's Well. This was piped to a conduit in the market place and grateful users undertook a yearly pilgrimage to the bishop's tomb to pray for the soul of their benefactor. The conduit and its bell were replaced in the 1790s but the gift of water was confirmed by Bishop Richard in 1803 'for the purpose of cleansing the town and, if occasion should require it, of extinguishing fires'. It still flows in conduits of blue lias along either side of the High Street.

In Frome an ancient leat channels hurrying spring water along the course of Cheap Street. It adds further charm to a thoroughfare lined with buildings which date back to the 16th and 17th centuries and which retain much of their period interest despite a terrible fire in 1923 and various alterations over the centuries. Chard has three major springs and the water from one of them,

Photo Roy Gallop

Resurrection Spring, is channelled along its main street. As the illustration in 'Wife for Sale' shows, Chard has added sculptures to further enhance the attraction of this feature.

The River Somer has been pleasantly canalised alongside the High Street in Midsomer Norton while in Nether Stowey a stream runs from the mill site beside the castle mound along Castle Street and then St Mary Street. Coleridge referred to its deep channel as his 'Dear Gutter of Stowey.' The stream that fed the mill at North Petherton still runs west to east beside the roads and pathways of that town too.

The drama of Cheddar Gorge is heightened by the waters of a huge underground river which emerge into daylight via eighteen separate springs below Pulpit Rock. As the Cheddar Yeo river they then flow down the gorge, beside The Cliffs and along a course which once fed no less then seven water-powered mills in the town.

Pictured here are, (facing page), Wells Market Place, and Midsummer Norton. Streams pictured on this page are at Nether Stowey, North Petherton and Cheddar.

Gloves and Gloving

I'm Burlington Bertie,
I rise at ten thirty and saunter along like a toff,
I walk down the Strand with my gloves in my hand,
Then I walk down again with them off.

Census figures for 1861 reveal that a third of the 25,300 glovers in England and Wales lived in Somerset. South Somerset, in particular, was one of the country's major glove producing areas. Yeovil was at the heart of this industry which, though now much reduced, still produces quality and specialist gloves. Yeovil Town's football team are known as 'The Glovers' and there is a Glovers Walk in the town's shopping centre.

Prior to the 13th century only the wealthy wore gloves but slowly they became a fashion item, especially after the restoration of the monarchy in 1660. The simpler styles of the past were then replaced by coloured materials and more elaborate designs. Gloves for women tended to be longer, sometimes reaching to the elbow, and were often enlivened by special stitching or other decoration. Men generally used leather gloves, women those of soft skins or fabric.

Gloves were, at one time, used to mark a transaction or service, often as rental payment for land. The sovereign marked the grant of a market by the giving of a pair of gloves which had to be displayed to validate the right to trade and the market bylaws. Plain gloves were a traditional gift for wedding guests and clergymen would expect a pair for officiating at a church ceremony or at the meal that accompanied the tithe payments. The Reverend Woodforde mentions a funeral where the principal mourners received a gift of 'black shammy' gloves and Pastor Holland complains of one where the next of kin failed to send him either 'hatband or gloves'.

Glove making began as a cottage industry with many small villages having their own tanner, cutter and sewers. As it grew the use of local sheep skins was supplemented by more exotic materials and the importation of hides and skins through London and Bristol. Until 1826 the industry was protected from foreign glove imports, except those smuggled in, so that high profits were made and contributed, along with those from wool and textiles, to funding the county's churches and charities.

In dozens of factories the parers, stakers, dyers and stainers passed their treated skins on to the cutters to prepare the glove pieces to specific hand sizes. These were than handed over to local outworkers for the sewing, pointing, buttonholing, finishing and decoration processes and then returned for boxing and despatch to London and overseas markets, especially in the colonies. In this way gloving provided a livelihood for a sizeable proportion of the population in many towns and villages. Children helped their mothers to supplement the family income and learn their skills, and some villages really hummed with the sound of sewing machines. Sometimes local shopkeepers or innkeepers acted as agents for collecting and delivering the work, and the payments for it (sometimes partly in goods, or even beer) influenced the whole rhythm of life in a gloving community.

The gloving industry witnessed great changes during the 19th century. The lifting of the import ban in 1826 was offset by rising demand and transport improvements which helped output to double between 1830 and 1860, but earlier tariff reductions were then followed by their complete abolition. To the calf and kid skins already coming in from Europe was now added an annual 6m pairs of finished gloves, especially the more elegant designs from France and some cheaper gloves from Germany, Italy and Austria.

Over the period to the end of the century glove output now slowly dropped back to its old level and became more concentrated. But gloves were still in demand. More were being used for work purposes in factories and on the farm, housemaids wore gloves for cleaning the better class homes, and riders and coachmen needed them for a good grip on the reins. There were countless names and styles and dandies thought nothing of wearing gloves dyed yellow, blue or lilac. Woollen and fabric gloves were everywhere but Somerset's leather specialisation helped it to supplant rival Worcester in terms of glove production.

Another effect of freer trade was to stimulate a degree of mechanisation to help counter the import challenge. Hot air, steam or gas were increasingly used to improve output and reduce costs in the factories and a simple form of sewing machine slowly replaced the 'donkey' and traditional hand sewing in outworkers' cottages. The proportion of one male to every five female glove workers in 1861 changed to a ratio of around 40:60 in 1901 and the proportion of outwork diminished. Some firms began to specialise more, others dropped gloving in favour of spats, gaiters and other such items, but the glove trade continued to be important in Somerset throughout most of the 20th century. At its beginning gloving was still a major employer and glove makers enjoyed a good standard of living but changing tastes, the effects of war and the rise of other industries continued to reduce the size and importance of the glove making activity. Thankfully not all of it disappeared, and today there are still several firms in Somerset to continue the centuries-old craft of making high class gloves.

The Lost Boys

The gravestones are already crumbling and now there is no living memory of these boys. They remain as ghosts in the fading records of the school.

Country churchyards provide intriguing glimpses of life in times past and St. Mary's parish church in Portishead is the starting point for a look at the short lives of some lost boys. These boys were once pupils at the Training Ship *Formidable* and some lie under the yew trees after lives as short as eleven years, the eldest being sixteen. The gravestones give few clues, just the names, ages and dates of death for most, and at least three of the boys are recorded as 'drowned'. This is unsurprising given that T S *Formidable* was their home, an Industrial Training School aboard a decommissioned naval ship moored in King Road off Portishead in the fierce tides of the Bristol Channel.

The Bristol training ship was founded in 1869 by a group of Bristolians which included Henry Fedden, chairman of the Board of Magistrates of one of the poorest districts of Bristol. He was deeply concerned about the number of destitute boys appearing at court. Records of the time show that the purpose of the training ship was to convert 'street arabs' into 'useful members of society'. The motto of the school 'Prevention is Better than Cure' reflects this ideal.

Henry Fedden was the honorary secretary for the training ship from its inception until his death in 1917 and he was supported in his efforts for the ship by some of the city's eminent families - the Wills' and Frys'. The memorial to Henry Fedden in the school's chapel is inscribed 'to him a poor boy was a sacred trust.'

Boys were mainly referred to the school by the courts after sentences of detention for 'wandering' or 'truancy' but often not charged with any offence. Boys were also sometimes transferred from institutions in other parts of the country if they had shown interest in going to sea. 'Volunteers' were boys paid for by friends or family so that they could be trained for a sea-going career,

Many of the boys sent from court had led grim lives of extreme poverty. Newspaper reports from the 1870s give a picture of barefoot, barely clad and underfed lads from homes lacking furniture or any amenity. Some had no homes and begged or scavenged for food, sleeping in whatever shelter they could find. "Under a cart," said one when asked where he slept. Most were not orphans but had parents who were unable to support their children because, even though they had work, they had insufficient money for food, decent housing or clothes. Of course some of these parents indulged in 'drink' to escape the grim reality of their lives and this was seen as the cause of their problems. For those boys brought by police officers or city missionaries to the court and sent to T S *Formidable* there was a chance to break out of this deprivation.

New recruits to the school were fitted out with a substantial wardrobe including 2 flannel shirts, 2 day shirts, 2 night shirts, 2 hose, 1 pair of shoes, 2 pairs of trousers, a cap with a ribbon inscribed with *FORMIDABLE* in gold lettering, a cravat and 2 handkerchiefs. Probably even more welcome were the three meals a day. Although the diet of bread, stews and porridge would seem monotonous to today's children the 'street arabs' must have felt that their luck had changed. Indeed, boys before the courts would often request to be sent to the *Formidable*.

'T S Formidable' moored in King Road, Portishead. This photograph shows the two decker 'Ship of the Line' with cut down rig. 300 pupils accommodated aboard ship received sea-going training aboard a two masted brig the 'Polly.' The 'school' came ashore in 1903 to a substantial building which eventually closed in the early 1980s and is now residential apartments known as Fedden Village.

In many ways life on board was good, especially when compared to the life which many boys had led previously. As well as the smart clothing and nutritious food, efforts were made to keep the pupils warm and healthy. For instance records show that 'warming apparatus' was purchased to heat the lower deck and there were baths and drying rooms. The ship could call upon the services of a medical officer who was a local doctor. He arranged regular health inspections and attended if staff or boys were ill. Boys were routinely vaccinated as early as 1871. All boys were trained in seamanship and basic literacy and numeracy. By 1876 training had expanded to include swimming, music (for the ship's band), carpentry, cooking, tailoring and shoemaking as well as geography and scripture.

At this time the majority of the boys left the school to serve in the Merchant Navy with a few entering the Royal Navy and even fewer the army, usually as a bandsman, or other land based work. On leaving boys were given a survival kit of blankets, a mattress, a chest, clothes and waterproofs.

The routine of the day was strict. The boys started cleaning the ship at 5.30am in summer and 6.30am in winter and worked until a breakfast of cocoa, bread and treacle at 7.30am Then there were schooling, seamanship or general duties until dinner time. This meal always included meat and vegetables and was followed by more schooling or duties until supper at 5.00pm of tea and bread. The day finished with 'turning in' at 8.0 pm unless boys were on 'night watch' duties.

Discipline was rigorous - meals were taken in silence and flogging with 'the ropes end' punished serious misdemeanors. This practice, which could inflict open weals on the skin, was replaced in 1872 by caning with the birch rod to a maximum of eighteen strokes. Boys could also be deprived of food or held in solitary confinement for up to forty-eight hours as punishment.

By 1878 H.M. Inspector of Schools reported 'the boys appeared to be in an improving condition of health...and order much improved. Punishment is decreasing in frequency and severity. Boys cheerful'... In 1882 the medical officer noted 'a wonderful improvement in physique of boys attributed to good diet with fresh vegetables and judicious muscular exercise especially swimming. Not one of the boys showed on his person any marks of punishment.' Home leave was rare, most boys had no home to go to. However there were occasional organised days away from the ship, the trip to the Clifton Zoological Gardens by boat and train being a highlight of the year.

From early days on *Formidable* the records show that there were serious drawbacks to life on board. The safety of the ship was never entirely secure with a catalogue of broken moorings and dragged anchors in response to gales and strong currents. Accommodation, although constantly repaired and regularly upgraded, was often leaking and damp. Staff as well as boys suffered illness associated with damp living conditions with several deaths attributed to respiratory disease. Victims included the chief officer, Mr. Bear, who died in 1873 of 'pleurisy and congestion of the lungs.'(In the earliest days of the training ship Mr Bear received the medal of the Humane Society for rescuing a boy who had fallen into the water.)

In 1872 an analysis of the drinking water on board found it 'very unsatisfactory' yet it took months, if not years, to purchase a suitable water carrying boat to remedy this. However there is no evidence that the ship ever experienced a serious epidemic. There were hazards in living on board a sailing ship and learning to handle the heavy sails and rigging. William Symes, described as being 'of very good character and a fine looking boy' died after falling from his hammock at the age of 12. Another boy, William Bray, admitted to the training ship at age 11, fell down the main hatch while playing and broke his neck, after just three months on board.

The most risky element in a life at sea is always the transfer between ship and shore when a simple missed footing can result in a ducking or even drowning. Such incidents were recorded almost casually as in this extract from the annual report of 1876:

'We have experienced deliverence from fire, and from accidents while moving our heavy weights, and while one boy, Thomas Maylam, has been drowned, we have in another case had five boys overboard at once, and again, the boats swamped in a heavy sea without loss of life.'

During this year the ship was stripped and rigging replaced and the medical officer Dr. Wigan reported (a month after Thomas Maylam's death), 'No epidemic, no very serious illness, no serious accident, no deaths'! In fact the records frequently failed to include references to deaths year by year or even in the individual records of each boy. The medical officer's report in 1876 says 'while we registered 3 deaths in the early part of the year, they hardly belong to the period to which this report refers - brain disease and atrophy having previously marked them out for this unavoidable result.'

A Jubilee year pamphlet of 1954 gives a short history of T S *Formidable*, which includes this fascinating extract:

'Life was hard on board but must be measured by the conditions of the 19th century. Reverend Charles Kingsley who was chief speaker at the opening ceremony had drawn attention to the plight of the naked climbing boys forced to wriggle through hot chimneys. 'Oliver Twist' and 'Nicholas Nickleby' stressed the conditions faced by boys in work-houses. Women and children were still working down mines. 71 boys died in the 44 years between 1869 and 1913. Some fell from rigging, some drowned and some died from disease. All were given a military funeral complete with gun carriage. Most survived and thrived.'

By comparison with the risks faced by most working class boys at the time, the boys of T S Formidable were well protected. The 'lost boys' named on the gravestones in St. Mary's churchyard were very small in number by comparison to the thousands of boys who graduated from the ship to lead the useful adult lives of the school's founders' aspirations ...but spare a thought for the young lives lost if you visit this peaceful churchyard.

This picture taken in 1871 shows a group of boys assembled amidships in the early days of T S Formidable.

Sources and Acknowledgements

With so many subjects covered, the sheer volume of sources consulted in the preparation of this volume makes it impossible adequately to mention them in detail. Much of the material was accumulated in the process of research for articles in the former *Somerset Magazine* and originated in the main county libraries, the record office and in the files of the *Somerset County Herald*. As explained in the Introduction the idea for this work stemmed from reading the volumes of the old *Somerset Year Book* and a large debt is owed to that publication not only for the concept itself but also for some of the information provided by its contributors over the years. *Somerset & Dorset Notes & Queries* issues have also touched on subjects like wife selling and the fives game. *The Victoria County History* is another useful background source as are the great Somerset records provided by early historians like Collinson and Phelps. The writers and publishers gratefully acknowledge all such sources and also the invaluable assistance and encouragement provided by David Bromwich of the Somerset Studies Library. Our thanks to Richard Burley, Chief Archivist of the Bristol Record Office. We acknowledge the typing services provided by Leighanne Gough. All photographs are by Geoff Body unless otherwise stated. Line drawings by Roy Gallop (who was kindly given permission by Taunton County Museum to sketch the shoes of the giant Joseph Sewell) except in the following cases:- Pages 1, 2 and 36 from W. H. Pyne's *Rustic Vignettes for Artists and Craftsmen;* Page 27 from *Woodcuts by Thomas Bewick and his School;* Page 35 from *Bristol Wagon & Carriage Works, (illustrated catalog 1900),* all published by Dover Publications. Inc. (New York); Page 33 reproductions from *Delineations of the north western division of the County of Somerset,* by John Rutter (1829), courtesy of Somerset Studies Library; Page 17 from *Master Roi and his School;* Page 45 photograph by kind permission of 'Memories', Old Photographic Prints, Corn Exchange, Bristol; Page 47 photograph supplied by Bristol Record Office by kind permission of Portishead Nautical Trust. The study on *Little Jack Horner*, page 16 was taken from the author's own book *Fussells Ironworks-Mells.*

LOOKING AHEAD to Volume 2.....

The strong hope of the compilers and publishers of Past Somerset Times is that the response to this first volume will warrant a continuation of the series. Our plans for a second volume are already quite well advanced with withies, beer and cider houses, early bathing, workhouses and many other such subjects scheduled for inclusion.

We intend to continue the practice of offering a special price to individuals, groups, societies, museums etc and a note or a call to Fiducia Press (address etc below) will ensure that you are sent advance information on further volumes in due course.

FIDUCIA AND KINGSMEAD BOOKS:-

SPECIALIST LOCAL BOOKS - available from good booksellers or by post from Fiducia Press,

10 Fairfield Road, Bristol BS3 1LG (telephone 0117 9713609 & 0117 9852795)

Fussells Ironworks, Mells (£5)	**Views of Labour and Gold** (£10)
The Glastonbury Canal (£5)	by William Barnes (1801 - 1886)
The Parrett Navigation (£4)	**Tracts from the Tracks** (£5)
The Coaching Era (£6.50)	(The Ridgeway Poems)
Exploring the Smaller Towns of Somerset (£6.95)	**Recollections of Jazz in Bristol** (£10)
The Severn Tunnel (£19.95)	(Foreword by Acker Bilk)
The Gentle Giants (£3) (Working Shire Horses)	**Dave Collett Blues** (£5)
Recollections of Chew Magna (£5)	**Manly Monodes** (£3.00)

All orders post free. Full list of titles sent on request.